FIRST STEPS ON
A SPIRITUAL PATH

First Steps
on a Spiritual Path

*White Eagle's Introduction
to the Inner Wisdom*

THE WHITE EAGLE PUBLISHING TRUST
NEW LANDS · LISS · HAMPSHIRE · ENGLAND

'Morning Light' first published 1957
Republished as 'First Steps on a Spiritual Path' with
revisions and a new introduction, September 2005
Reprinted March 2009

© The White Eagle Publishing Trust, 1957, 2005

British Library Cataloguing-in-Publication Data
A catalogue record for this book is available
from the British Library

ISBN 978-0-85487-162-9

Typeset in 11.5 on 15pt Baskerville at the Publishers
and printed and bound by Universal Packaging (Pvt) Ltd,
77 Nungamugoda Rd, Kelaniya, Sri Lanka

CONTENTS

v

INTRODUCTION

THE PATH that a person walks through life is individual. A true spiritual teaching recognises that each one of us is uncovering his or her own wisdom, his or her own approach to truth; and therefore such a teaching simply casts light to illumine the way. The wisdom which has come from White Eagle and is contained in this book does just this. It offers the reader the opportunity to set their earthly, human experience against the patterns of the vast sky above; to see them in the context of the wider world that is spirit.

In keeping with the idea of 'shedding light', this book (originally compiled some time ago) was first called MORNING LIGHT. 'Light' because the teaching contained in this book sheds light on what is often a 'shadowy' world, and 'morning' to imply that the advice given has a freshness to it, the beginning of a glorious day.

It is not absolutely vital to know who White Eagle is in order to be helped by this book. It will, however, be obvious that he speaks from the world of spirit. Those who read the book will find that he tries to help us create a bridge in order to bring together what we might call cosmic understanding (the wordless wisdom of the divine mind) and the wisdom that comes from human experience. His teaching gives us a broader perspective: we realise that there is great value in treading the simple human road that we do, but that with spiritual illumination, nothing that once felt heavy or painful ever has quite the same hold on us. Illumination is release.

White Eagle—his words have come to us through the earthly medium of Grace Cooke—regards himself as a messenger for a Brotherhood in spirit, and no more. The men and women who comprise the Brotherhood of the Star are simply those who have been treading the path of incarnation a little longer than the rest of us. These are the ones that guide, the ones who bring about miracles in human lives; some of those miracles are described in this book. Many of these souls have moved beyond incarnation, or are able to move in and out of incarnation at will. These are masters, and mastery, in White Eagle's teaching, is the goal of every soul.

Behind all of White Eagle's teaching is the symbol of the Star—six-pointed, and shining with light. It is representative of many things, not least of which is our own perfected form, the being after which we all strive. If there is one thing that White Eagle would encourage us to do for our happiness, it is to keep our vision on the Star, the image of our perfection. In doing so, we may grow into our Star self, and then light will truly shine from us all.

JCH

I

Gleam of Dawn

WE COME from the life of spirit, a life beyond death, to bring you a message which will give you spiritual help, which will comfort and heal and bring peace to your hearts; a message which will answer some of the problems which confuse you at the present day. For the outer world is in turmoil, and the minds of men and women agitated by fear, distrust, anger, and resentment. Humanity can find no answer to its problems, because instead of looking to the Source of absolute wisdom, men and women endeavour to answer all questions purely with their mental or intellectual powers, or else on the material level of life.

The answer to every human problem lies in the Divine Mind; and when human beings can rise above themselves and contact the Divine Mind, then they will receive the guidance for which they long. Our purpose is to help you to make this contact, and thus to find the true guidance, the true answer to the problems which perplex you.

We have spoken many times of the great need for each individual to understand that he or she has an inner, spiritual existence as well as an outer, worldly life; and it is essential that each should discover that spiritual part, and set himself or herself to develop it. There are many schools of teaching, but only one central truth of which all else is but a part, and this truth is pure spirit. You have this pure spirit within your own being, and you are here on earth to develop your spiritual self—which is in truth the Son of God, the Christ Being, lying buried beneath many coverings, physical, mental and emotional.

Do you not understand that within you is something more precious, more beautiful, more wonderful than anyone has ever conceived? Occasionally you hear stories of a manifestation of that glory through the saints or great ones; you see through them the radiance of the divine life. You think to worship, but never to draw near these great ones. You worship from afar, instead of taking hold of yourself and working to perfect your own character and your own soul so that they become fitted for the divine spirit to manifest through you to your fellow creatures. Yet this is the whole purpose of your life.

We have said that people try to solve all the problems of the age from a purely material standpoint, and because of this they are filled with fear: fear for themselves, fear of and for their companions. In the new Aquarian age towards which you are all advancing, there will be stimulation of both the spiritual and material aspects of the human being. A number of souls are already in incarnation who either consciously or unconsciously have come here to be pioneers of the new age.

We would therefore have you understand that however simple, however obscure your own life may appear, you have a special mission or charge. You have come to earth for a special purpose, not only to develop your own divine consciousness, but also as a pioneer to serve the coming age.

You cannot help but develop your own character, your own innate divinity, if you do not trouble too much about your own growth or development, and instead truly serve your brothers and sisters on earth. For when once a soul learns to recognize and obey spiritual laws, it will find itself following a spiritual pathway, which seems to be already opened and prepared for it. This happens with all pioneers of the spirit, although many of these are passing through a hard time, for they have necessarily to work in comparative solitude to prepare for an influx of many of the brethren of the Christ Star, souls who are presently coming to the earth. Angels too will draw near and men will walk and talk with angels. But remember, it takes an angel to recognize an angel, a god to recognize a god; so that until humanity has developed the necessary qualities within, people as a whole remain unconscious of the presence of angels or of gods.

Truth lies within Yourself

If you would find an answer to every personal or world problem, practise the art of becoming very still within—as still and silent as the surface of a lake without a breath of wind to disturb it. This lake represents your soul, and when it is still and you have developed the will of God within yourself, then you will see without distortion the reflection of truth on the waters of the lake which is your soul or 'psyche'. 'Be still, and know that I am God!'. When a soul is alone with God, God speaks to it. The individual then sees truth reflected in his or her own psyche. But if the person does not use the *divine* will, does not pray for the will of God to be done; if people are willful, seeking an answer in accord with their own desires, then the answer will be distorted, for there is no peace in any of them, the lake of their souls is not still.

The soul of each man and woman is a wonderful instrument, and can be likened to a radio receiver with which the person can tune in to many stations; either to spheres in the grey lower astral worlds of disquiet and desire, or to spheres where all life is a manifestation of the beauty of God; and even, if the person so desires, to other planets of the solar system. The human being has indeed been given wings, but has yet to learn how to unfold these wings and rise into worlds of infinite beauty.

In your prayers and aspirations, you may touch a vibration of purity that you feel in your heart as simple goodness. Such a pure feeling as this does not depend upon possession of a powerful and well-stored mind, but upon a pure and constant joy uprising in the heart. Every son or daughter of the living God should live joyfully. If you analyze our words, you will find they are profoundly true. Take as an example your own life. If you were touching the secret of joy, and recognized and faithfully cherished in your life this pure joy in God, how different your feelings and outlook would be!

Think of the immense blessing conferred upon humankind by the soul who can live in joy and pure goodness without any thought of the result to self. The ideal, of course, is to do right because you love the right, because the joy within you, the life of the spirit within you, cannot do other than express itself as goodness.

Have you ever thought that only the goodness

of individual men and women safeguards the future of the race? If there were no goodness in the world, there would be no future for humanity. The man or woman who lives in singleness of purpose to do good, to be good, to live happily, makes an enormous gift to generations yet unborn. Nevertheless, we recognize that it is not easy to do good, or even to be good yourself just for the sake of goodness alone. Please believe that we do not preach at you; we are only trying to work out a certain theme which we can presently make clearer. Again and again, we say that if you can establish a foundation of joy and serenity within yourself, and express goodness in every action and in life itself, your contribution to the happiness of humankind will be beyond your power to estimate.

This can be illustrated by the life of Jesus. If you could only learn about that life in more detail, grasping its simplicity and humility; if you could realize his continual outpouring of the magical white light of heaven to help and heal, you would understand that only joy and goodness can truly release this power of the white magic. Any similar life is by its very nature continually pouring forth a divine essence.

This fact has been demonstrated by other great teachers. The yogis of the East have also discovered the source of all true happiness and the secret of a richer life. The continual service they pour forth to humankind does not seem like labour to them.

Rather is it a spontaneous and constant outpouring of divine essence.

Humanity's Great Descent

The human race has a wonderful journey before it. Humanity has already travelled far. Each soul has come forth as an unconscious but still potentially divine spark from the centre, the Godhead. It has descended through spheres of life invisible to people of the present day, down and down, ever taking on denser and heavier clothing, until at last it finds itself robed in the weightiest garment it will ever know—not only the body of dense flesh but also the material environment and existence, which will weight it down to the ground.

The substance of the earth itself has also been crystallizing, solidifying as it descended in the scale of vibrations, so that now both the human soul and spirit and the earth itself have touched the bottom of a descending arc.

Some ardent souls on earth are already climbing again towards the heights, but many are still undergoing the process of gradual descent or materialization. This knowledge may give us forbearance, and make us more patient with some of our companions.

During its journey down through the various planes of conscious existence, the soul has lived in states of beauty and harmony undreamed of today. That is why legends of Atlantis and even more remote eras have come down to us. People then inhabited bodies of a lighter, finer texture, and their souls were serene and joyous in an Eden-like world. They were like children still in contact with their heavenly Father and Mother, still remembering those Elysian Fields of happiness that they had left on their long journey into the depths of matter.

In the beginning, the human being was born, or *breathed* forth from the Holy of Holies, or from the 'womb' of Love, Wisdom and Power. People were then entirely pure and innocent of soul. Now they are destined to learn to conquer weakness, to control matter, to overcome temptation. That is why you are here.

In this connection, the story or legend of Atlas—who carried the world on his shoulders—is still significant; for it pictures the soul taking upon itself all the weight of worldliness. This burden is laid upon everyone; a burden that gradually increases until at the lowest arc of its evolution the soul is completely weighed down. At this stage it seems to be quite unaware of spheres of beauty and truth from which it came forth and to which it will eventually return.

World conditions today are again challenging the innate goodness enshrined in every human being, the goodness which is stimulating men and women to turn their faces upwards to receive the heavenly light. They have to realize that all the secrets of the universe are hidden within the individual being, waiting for him or her to release them.

II

The Miracle of Light

YOU HAVE asked us why the Divine Creator has decreed that every soul must leave a land of heavenly bliss to journey down into the world; and why that individualized soul, like the soul of Everyman, must presently and by its own effort struggle back again to the heavenly places? You believe that if you knew the reason for your suffering and limitation, it would give you a new incentive and purpose.

Naturally there is a purpose when souls breathed forth by the Creator are directed down through the spheres to this dark earth—a very grand purpose. When each individual at last glimpses the Plan for the spiritual nurture and evolution of God's child—himself or herself—that one will live in peace and patience; for then his or her soul will rise to touch again the fringe of heaven. We can never over-emphasize the reality and constancy of the divine love and care of God for each human soul: the wonderful, all-enfolding love that is far beyond all earthly understanding. It is a paradox that because of this very love the little spark of the human soul is sent forth on its long journey earthwards.

For if the soul did not descend into the darkness of matter it might never become conscious of itself or of its latent powers, or ultimately conscious of its God. This, in a few simple words, explains the real purpose of the soul's journey, for under pressure from the darkness of earth in time it gradually opens, as a seed sown in the soil does under rain, warmth and sunlight. In other words, the pressure of so-called hardness, stress and evil working upon that seed (or soul) forces growth from the unconscious into the conscious state. Through many ages, it grows and becomes ultimately master of matter, master of itself; and fully conscious, in matter, of the light and love of God.

So far as this earth plane is concerned, the soul must master its weaknesses, both of the flesh and the emotions; it must do so because it is essential to its purpose. When it has learned self-mastery, then at last it is free, it has become fully God-conscious, and so become at-one with the Creator, while yet on earth.

So you will see that there is indeed a purpose, a grand plan in the hands of the Great Architect of the Universe, a plan which is detailed and beautiful in order and design. You must learn to have patience and confidence in God.

Should you suffer any injustice, real or apparent, always try to remember that all human life is governed by divine love and divine law, and there is no innocent or wanton suffering. You appear to suffer unjustly, but only because you have yet to develop clear vision or clairvoyance—which can reveal your past and future. Until you have done so, you cannot recognize the outworking of spiritual law which is taking place, or see the play of unseen forces upon your being; nor can you understand the setting in which you—a jewel from the Father's crown—have been placed.

No-one can escape either the joy or pain, which he or she has earned. You are like magnets; and like magnets you attract to yourself that which is yourself. This is inescapable law. In other words, you attract to yourself conditions similar to those which you constantly create within yourself, and which you are ever externalizing from yourself.

Because life is governed by a law that is always just, perfect and true, there cannot be any injustice. This you will question; but when you see things in clearer perspective, you will perceive that every event in your life comes to influence your soul or to unfold your character, and that all is working together *in you* to bring forth the perfect son or daughter of God.

Out of the ashes of the old life arises the new life. This is what the symbol of the phoenix indicates. This mythical bird was in earlier symbology called the white eagle.

The perfect man or woman, the master soul, is a very wonderful and glorious being. You are that being, *in embryo:* perhaps, whenever you can remember this, your human life will seem truly worthwhile?

On Miracles

You have often read about the miracles performed by Jesus and by other initiates; and you may probably agree that certain happenings in your own lives can only be termed miraculous. It is true: miracles are still happening. And why not? *'As it was in the beginning, is now, and ever shall be.'* Such so-called miracles are manifestations of the power of the Light. When you better understand how the divine Light can work through and then control darkness, you will better understand how and why miracles occur.

An initiate* in time reaches a stage when he is beyond the limiting power of matter. He then becomes free to manifest through the ethers and the lie elements of earth, air, fire, and water. To illustrate this: the Old Testament tells how three prophets once

* An initiate is one who has become fully aware of the inner light.

walked through fire. Today also we have fire walkers, men of the East particularly, who can tread on red or white-hot ashes without injury to themselves. The materialistic ascribe this feat to some trick; the better-informed say it is due to self-hypnotism! Nothing, however, destroys the fact that these people have walked through fire unharmed. The reason we give, before coming to a deeper explanation, is that the operator, having attained a degree of mastery over the atoms of his body, can transmute or raise them until they become impervious to heat.

Much the same explanation applies to walking on water, which Jesus demonstrated. Not only did he do this, but he was able so to quicken the vibrations of Peter that he also walked on the water. But you will remember that immediately the disciple's faith wavered, he began to sink, and called to his Master to save him—which immediately he did.

Our point is that the Master had reached a degree of spiritual realization where he saw his body as composed of light, and not as a solid mass (as do most people); and because he was resolutely holding this thought, the body became so light that it could walk on water.

The transport of an initiate from one place to another by seemingly miraculous powers is not infrequent in the East. You may find this difficult to understand with your outer mind, but once you open your consciousness to higher realms of life, you will understand the law that enables the initiate to move his or her body at will in this manner.

The human body has also power to pass through matter. We do not, of course, seek to lessen the wonder of the miracles of Jesus when speaking of those performed by other initiates. He himself said, *The works that I do, shall ye do also*. He came to teach the world that same truth which we ourselves are inadequately trying to express. All that the glory of the spiritual sunlight, shining through Jesus, was able to accomplish will be done by all God's children when once they can fulfil the demands of the spiritual law.

Let us try to state this law in very simple words. All life consists of two aspects, which can be variously called positive and negative, constructive and destructive, light and darkness, good and evil. The two are in a way antagonistic. Everyone reacts to their influence, and feels their attraction and impulse. To illustrate this, your heart, which is your true self, longs for and believes in truth, believes in a heaven world, in Jesus Christ, and in God's goodness; it accepts these as a little child does, feeling and knowing that they are true. Another part of you is of the earth, and pulls you down again, so that what you may believe in tonight, tomorrow you cannot spare time for.

The whole purpose of your life down here is that

the spirit, your spirit, shall shine within earth's darkness. Your spirit is identical with the light that shone in the beginning. In the beginning of your existence, you were light; and the light shone in the darkness—which is your dense body on the earth—and the earth comprehended it not. You are familiar with these words, but you apply them to ages past, instead of to your own life. You do not understand that in essence you are light, a child of light. But your physical body, or what some call the mortal mind, cannot comprehend this light. You, the real you, are here for a purpose, to shine through both body and mind and transmute them. When the spirit gains control over matter, over the body, miracles happen. As the spirit becomes strong in its manipulation of physical atoms, it is able to use any of the elements at will.

This is not done by human thinking, but by the quickening of a pure spiritual consciousness in humanity, which is all love. This means the arising, or the coming to life of the Christ spirit in every human being, which says, *I am the light of the world!* And again, *In the beginning was the Word, and the Word was with God, and the Word was God.... And God said, Let there be light: and there was Light.*

Light is spiritually another word for life—for human life, all life. Pure light was the beginning of all creation. It is also the sustaining power of creation, the foundation of all things. Your own body,

24

seen with the eye of the spirit, is a form composed of clear light.

Many will presently be helped to realize this by science, which has now concluded that not only is there no solidity in matter—a truth which was known long, long ago by the sages—but has almost determined that physical matter does not really exist, that it is what in Sanskrit is called *maya* or illusion. We are told, however, that when the physical atom, with its electrons and protons, is examined by the eye of the spirit, it is seen that around the protons are particles of light. Thus within the physical atom the light shines, and without that light, there would be no atom, and no world in which man could exist.

Here then is a simple basic explanation of how and why miracles take place. They come about because of men and women developing this inner light, the light which is not only something which beautifies and illumines his heart, but a reality which permeates the very flesh which clothes his soul. It dwells within the very substance of physical matter, which the initiate controls by means of this realization. This light will shine through, control and glorify matter. Even thus do you glorify your Father–Mother who is in heaven.

All this may be beyond you at present, but it is your eventual goal. It means that you must not seek to escape from life with its hardships, except by making a stronger contact with God. Let God's light so suffuse your being that you are raised from darkness to light, from earth to heaven.

We say again that if you will try to purify your own bodily atoms by right thinking, right living, right feelings and actions, and by judging no-one but yourself, you will raise your whole consciousness and find happiness at present beyond your dreams. Peace will rule in your heart, and a gentle and gracious power in you will make crooked places straight.

Yes, the stories of miracles contain a deep esoteric truth. They illustrate the meaning of the Master's teachings. Study the scriptures; then study the human life around you with a loving eye. Study the immensity of the heavens. Love God. Seek the inner planes of your spiritual self frequently. Follow the inner light and the path of the spirit, and you will behold the mysteries of heavenly places. Then you will clearly understand how miracles are wrought.

III

The Quickening Sun

WE SHALL speak often about the qualities and nature of the light. By 'Light', we mean the Christ within human hearts, which manifests in the God-like qualities of gentleness and patience in a soul of hope, trust, forgiveness, intuitive sympathy with others, restraint and forbearance, and the quality of pure love from which all these arise. This is why we say, 'Love is light, and light is love'.

Worship of the Light

Long ago, we used to do all our planting of crops in accord with the light. That is to say, we invoked the blessing of the Great White Spirit on the seeds before they were planted. We directed the light into the earth itself. When people learn to do this again they will reap much finer crops with which to nourish both the body and the soul.

In ancient days, people were well aware of

these truths, well aware that light and love could be a power in the land. They would meet either in small bands or gather in vast ceremonies in order to worship the light. They were first taught how to do this by God-beings who in the beginning came to instruct their younger brethren in such arts. People learnt that the light that came to illumine their ways was a creation of the goodness of God; and that this light would ultimately reveal to all their homeward path to God.

Before the ceremonies, the ancient people would perambulate their 'lodge', would march with rhythmic steps and sacred song. This ceremony would take place on a level place, often on a hilltop. Throughout the night, they would pace around their vast temple, under an open sky lit by a myriad stars and planets in this solar system, both seen and unseen—for there are planets circling the sun which are unknown to humanity. All present understood that their worship was directed by angels of the light gathered for that purpose, and indeed visible to many. At the first light of dawn a great stillness came upon the multitude. Then at the first sight of the sun all the people turned to the light, worshipping, praising, thanking the Great White Spirit for the coming of a new day of special grace and blessing.

How many today would make time or opportunity to assemble to see the sun rise? How *many* could see the angelic hosts manifest in the sunrise and all the shining ones gathered to bless the peoples of the earth? Few indeed, we think. But long ago the peoples realized that at such times they were touching the secret of the creation of life, and were receiving into their being a radiation of the Solar Logos by which they were strengthened and purified. They *breathed* in the Light, which was actual life-force, and which purified, perfected, irradiated humankind.

The ancient people inhabited bodies of a finer vibration than that of the physical form of today, in the sense that they were more attuned to the forces of nature, to the great Mother God; more open to the spiritual forces, more open to the Light.

What is meant when it is said that a person bears a light within him- or herself? How does that person behave? Surely, as a child of God. According to his or her understanding, that person is true to God. The one who bears the light within must be true: such a person is a true man or woman. He or she must be true, because he or she sees clearly. His or Her vision is not distorted, not veiled. He sees and goes straight to truth, and gains ever freserh understanding of truth.

By this we see that the word 'light' must itself be another term for truth. Throughout the ages, it is said, God has never left human beings without a witness. Always, God has sent messengers to speak truth to humanity. Therefore we shall find in all races, past and present, something of this teaching concerning the Light. It was known during the Hyperborean Age, known by those who dwelt in the Andes, in Polynesia, in ancient Egypt and the Far East, and indeed right up to the early Christian era.

'Let the light shine!' was the command of the Egyptian high priest. 'Let the fire be lighted!' was the invocation of the high priest in the Andes; in Atlantis we find the same invocation, *'Let* the light shine!' as the priest of the great Sun Temple opened the worship. In the temples of Greece, the same command was voiced. Here the temple maidens or vestal virgins were given the task of guarding a flame upon the altar, emblematic of the sun. If the light ever went out their penalty was death.

Later we come to the advent of the Solar Logos, or the Christ who spoke through the lips of Jesus, saying, *I am the light of the world.*

The Christ Radiance

We remind you that the opening words in the Gospel of John declare, *The light shineth in darkness; and the darkness comprehended it not.* Few people stop to meditate upon and to contemplate the beauty contained in this saying. At the beginning of creation God said,

'Let there be light!' and out of the darkness the Light shone. The destiny of every individual human being is to attain full understanding of and have his or her being within the light of God.

When you dispose by fire of the outworn garment of a person's body of flesh after death, this disposal by fire means a changing of its atoms; or, in other words, a releasing of the light which was imprisoned within the atoms by the darkness. Indeed, what people fear as death is in truth a form of initiation of greater or lesser degree; at death a great light breaks upon the soul. My children, we beg you never to regard the passing of any soul from its imprisoning body into a richer life as something to be dreaded. According to the law of God, when the right time has come, the soul* goes forth, not to lose its identity but to gain a greater consciousness of God, and of the eternal light.

Thus, when one of you begins to understand the nature of light, when he or she can receive the radiation of the light, his or her Christ-consciousness is

*The word soul, if properly understood, means the person himself, or herself. This is the familiar 'ourself' of feelings, likes, dislikes, interests, affections, memories, and sentiments. In a word, it is the 'we ourselves' who live inside the outer being, and look out through its eyes, speak with its tongue and lips and think with its brain. It is this 'ourself' which survives death and migrates to a brighter realm.

stimulated. This person need not be over-intellectual or clever in order to respond. Only a simple loving person is required—that is all.

For in the degree that any person learns to practise loving kindness towards other human beings, or loves life itself as he or she finds it expressed in the beauty of every day, so does that person's light shine, because Christ radiates from him or her. Love, thus expressed, is drawing to the soul the sunlight of Christ, so that the truly loving soul becomes radiant.

For a moment, try to contemplate the face, the form, the appearance, and the whole nature of Jesus the Christ. We do not deny that there have been other world teachers who have received the light of Christ in great measure; but we hold before your vision now the great saviour of Christendom, Jesus the Christ. See in him the divinity of God, the purity and beauty of the Christ spirit; see how Jesus expressed the full glory of the Christ love; for the Christ love is Light.

Then for a moment try to imagine what heaven itself is like. Try to create heaven according to your own idea. Try to imagine a state of being constantly irradiated by golden light. See in that heavenly state beings, perhaps angelic, perhaps human. One and all will seem to you as if lighted from within, for all are radiating light. Why is it that spirit people who come back from their celestial state appear as beings of light? Why is this heaven so suffused with light?

Because, in its reality, life is light.

Then read in your Bible of the visitation of angels as seen by prophets and saints of old. Was not Paul smitten by a great light, and utterly changed? Angels, clothed in brightness, appeared to minister to Peter. Jesus once withdrew with three disciples to a hilltop, where he and even his raiment became transfigured by the glory of the light.

These are stories told by honest and true men. They happened only yesterday, so recent is two thousand years ago in comparison with the history of humanity. Do you believe these things? They are still happening, and will always do so, because behind all physical form is a spiritual life-force which expresses itself as light.

Again and again we say, *Light is life, and life is light.* For people to retain light within they must *love.* Look at anyone you know who is loving and kind. See how a light shines through. Try yourself to see whether you can observe love expressed in other faces, even the unlikely kind of face. Alas, when someone does not love he or she becomes charged with self-pity. This lets down the shutters of his or her soul. Then the person looks dark, for their light is subdued or even covered up.

So: let the light shine! Send out the light! Go about life with a loving attitude, and your light will indeed be bright.

Do you know that the life-force derived from Light and coursing through your veins is the secret of perfect health? Yes, lack of light means lack of certain elements in the bloodstream, which will eventually cause disease, sickness, and breakdown. Jesus knew this secret. He knew well how to receive the radiation from the Son of God. He did not need to touch the body of a sick person to send light into that body, for he had overcome limitations of time and space. When the centurion came to Jesus begging that his servant might be healed, Jesus had already extended his aura and healed the sick man by infusing him with vibrations of light. In other words, he took light into the darkness and dispelled it.

Light infuses even the substance of the earth. You think of your earth as dark, as dead, but in the substance of the earth, her physical matter, there is light.

The very life of God expresses itself as light; and this light sustains the mortal life in a human body and eventually gives eternal life to a human soul. The real object of human life, therefore, is to discover and to make use of light, and thus become a 'sun' or son (or daughter) of God. Probably you are by now thinking that you have a long way to go. So have we all. But we who speak have *seen;* we know that life is essentially light, and the perfect life is the glory of God.

Be patient. Look forward, and never back. Turn your faces to the light and 'keep on keeping on' patiently and trustingly. In the degree that you give forth light, which is love, you will assuredly receive. Be encouraged, and not disheartened. If you are sad or suffering, we pray that you may have a demonstration of the power of God's light and love to work miracles, both in your body and your material circumstances. The law is this: God has so created His–Her sons and daughters that *they themselves must release* the light before it can act in them, and in their outer lives.

Look ever to the Light, which shall overcome all shadow and set you free. Such a freedom means peace of mind and heart, happiness, and abundance of all that is needed. The time is approaching when human beings will be able to command the action of light over matter, and do this unselfishly for the good of all.

IV

The Light that is Life

THINK OVER these things often. Your Bible affirms that God 'created man in His own image'. This is indeed true. Even with your present limited understanding you can recognize God as omnipotent, omniscient and omnipresent; and one and all of you have had demonstrations of love and wise guidance that have convinced you of an intelligent and loving Power behind your life.

Sometimes, of course, this Power has directed you into situations that you dislike, and you suffer because you decide that things have gone wrong; that nothing you wished to happen has occurred. But when you become more enlightened you will no longer see things in this way. You will know that God's laws are just, perfect and true, and that whatever happens in your outer life, however undesirable it may seem to the outer mind, has always a compensating blessing behind it.

When you have been relieved of a former condition to which you were clinging, this is like a parent releasing from a baby's fingers a plaything in which the parent sees harm or danger; the baby screams, but the wise mother gently says, 'No, my child, here is something better'; and offers her baby something more suitable.

Apply this illustration to your own life and its happenings, and you will learn in time the value of acceptance. Try to accept what happens, knowing that God is wise in all His–Her giving, and perhaps even wiser in withholding or taking away. The whole point is that when the human soul evolves and expands in consciousness of God it cannot really lose anything. Only its own limited consciousness prevents the soul from recognizing that *all is here, all is present.*

People who spend much time in prayer, or meditation on God are sometimes misunderstood by their companions, who say that action is better than prayer. True, action is right at the right time, but action should result from meditation and prayer, and never from emotional stress.

The Elder Brethren

Now we would like to tell you about the Elder Brethren, men and women who live on the heights. By 'heights' we mean an elevation of consciousness as well as remote mountainous places of the earth. These Brethren have reached a level of spiritual knowledge on which they are in close communion with the Eternal Spirit; and from this level they work unceasingly for the spiritual illumination and unfoldment of humanity. Being attuned to God, their own soul-consciousness expands so that they become attuned to all human life; and in this exalted state they become messengers between the Creator and His–Her creatures.

They still retain their physical form as men and women, and having passed through all grades and degrees of human life, they understand the most elementary need of any human being. They are all love and understanding. They are never severe, nor do they coerce; they leave their younger brethren in absolute freedom of choice. They worship God constantly, and through that worship radiate light and love to humanity. The majority of people do not recognize this influence radiated by these great ones; nevertheless it is constantly at work. Thus the Elder Brethren work ceaselessly for you and all people.

They are never hasty, never judge anyone. The young in soul are quick to judge, but the Brethren are patient, for they are well aware how slow is the process of soul-expansion in any of God's creatures. They never expect too much of anyone. These Elder Brethren are very close to humanity. As soon as an individual learns to use divine law, to act by divine law, then the channel opens wide to the inflowing power of the Christ light.

The World Teacher

It is frequently asked if another World Teacher is soon to come. But you realize of course that there can be only the one supreme Son of Life? In Christianity he is called Jesus Christ. Through Jesus of Nazareth, the light once shone; through other initiates the same light will some day shine, but on a higher spiral, a higher cycle of life.

You are probably wondering whether the World Teacher will be recognized or accepted by church or people when he appears? We wonder, for this does not always happen. Only from a distance, sometimes after the lapse of centuries, is recognition given. We have to remember always that it is not the *person* of that World Teacher which is significant, but the radiation of the Christ light which shines through him or her. In course of time, the world will begin to wonder and to worship when it sees the power and influence radiated by the life of this great being, and when it realizes the wisdom of his–her teachings.

The World Teacher draws very close to humanity at the present time, and brings all love, all wisdom. The mighty power and light of the Teacher will stimulate the subtler bodies of all people; indeed, that influence is already active upon earth. This is why you see so many international difficulties and upheavals, and many a clash of ideologies; one nation wants to do one thing, one another, so that humanity is apt to behave like children in a nursery. People react to the stimulation of this great spiritual light in different ways: why, they do not understand. They feel a tremendous urge to push forward, to assert themselves, a desire to introduce brotherhood in its crudest form. Behind all such immature expressions of unrest and quickening is the impulse proceeding from the coming light of the World Teacher.

Do not think about him or her as being represented by one individual only. While heavenly light and power will shine through the Teacher, its inflow will not be confined to the one personality alone but will be working like leaven in the bread. It will stimulate the spirit in people, and will also quicken the vibrations of the earth itself.

The World Teacher, when he or she comes to earth, will not descend alone, but will bring many disciples. Many are indeed already here, working to prepare against that coming. Some of you may be of that number. Disciples are used to quicken the vibrations, to lighten the darkness in readiness for the greater manifestation.

Every one of you has to be raised before you can understand spiritual truth or reality. The disciples already labour to prepare the way. When at last Everyman is ready, he will in truth raise his eyes to behold the dawning light.

Human memory is very fallible and often needs reminding of truths vital to its being. You often forget your destiny, the path on which your feet are set.

You also forget that you are far more than merely a physical body and mind, and that you will not, cannot die. You will not even know when your own moment of death takes place, for you will find yourself exactly the same person when you have stepped out of your body as before. The kingdom of heaven does not mean some far-distant country to which you will go when you have shed your body. It is here with you, now; and you are here on earth encased in matter to earn by your labour the equipment you will need to make your own road into that glorious heavenly state, which can only be achieved by your own effort and spiritual unfoldment.

You have been told that if you truly believe in the Lord Jesus Christ he will as truly save you. Yes indeed; but not without your own effort and co-operation, your own work upon yourself and your environment. For is it not said that whatsoever a man soweth he shall surely reap?

Your thoughts, words and deeds are the seeds you are daily sowing all your life through. The result of this sowing is certain and inescapable. We do not preach, or try to frighten anyone; we are just giving you truth, which you can prove for yourselves very easily. If things are difficult for you tomorrow morning and you allow yourself to get upset about them, life will seem very unpleasant. If, on the other hand, you remember that the things of earth are not all-important, you will remain happy. If you are hasty, you will get into difficulties; but if you are patient and calmly look to God for the directions you need, then all will be well.

Your thoughts and actions are like seeds, the harvest of which is certain to be reaped at some time, in the soul as well as in the bodily life; and will also shape your whole future. This is an expression of the perfect law and is inescapable.

Together with this law (sometimes called *karma*) is a complementary law that the East calls *dharma*. Now *dharma* means that an opportunity is always given by which you can make the best of all circumstances and conditions, by realising that they come to offer you an opportunity to express your highest and best. Therefore, together with the law of cause and effect—strict, just, perfect and true—there is also the law of *dharma*, which demonstrates God's mercy. Assuredly, God is ever merciful to His–Her child, but never promises that the child shall not have to work, or suffer, or will evade expiating its sins. Instead, God is saying, 'My child, my love is with you and will help you'. God's love is God's mercy. God can thus heal

42

all wounds by helping the children of God to pass through their self-created karma. This mercy of God is closely related to the mercy of men and women. In the degree that one of you shows mercy to your companions, so does God release mercy to you.

We have touched on the power of Christ to save souls. The Christ light within is indeed your only saviour. God has endowed every one of His–Her children with the Christ spirit, which is the saving grace of life. In this manner, Christ will save all who dwell in ignorance and sin. The divine law is love, and to break that law is sin. By reason of the discomfort and pain caused by such a violation, the soul eventually gains wisdom. Ignorance of divine law is however no excuse for sin.

On the soul's path of unfoldment, service to others is of the first importance. This can be given on the inner planes as well as the outer. The first service of any soul is of necessity to God, and is expressed in worship and adoration; the second law is to love your neighbour as yourself.

Service through Worship

This brings back the thought of the Elder Brethren, who spend their lives in worshipping, in adoring, in meditation upon God. By this act they are helping the whole of humanity, and refining the substance of the earth herself. Any quickening of the spiritual life of men and women does this. The Elder Brethren radiate an influence which is surely, although slowly, permeating both humanity and mother earth. In the same way, all who truly worship and praise God are serving humankind.

The greatest of God's gifts is human life itself; and the fact that you can daily grow in awareness of a purer life, more harmonious and beautiful than anything yet known upon earth.

This also entails your having faith in the unseen influences and in these unseen brothers and sisters who are ever close to you in spirit when you prepare yourself to receive them. My children, if you would only sit quietly with minds stilled, meditating upon heavenly things, you would be inviting the unseen guest, the elder brother or sister; you would feel his or her influence.

What we tell you is true. The Brethren of the White Light work to help you. They are ever with you. They turn your thoughts upward. Seek first the Kingdom. Seek first the contact with the Infinite Spirit. Seek only to worship and glorify your Creator. Then you can be likened to a candle light, very simple and unassuming; but countless candle lights held up to God increase even God's light and glory. You cannot live to yourself or for yourself. You are living to God; and as you grow, so do God's light and power increase. Why did God create you in the first instance? Because God gives out continual joy and life, and eventually receives back joy and life from His–Her children. What a grand opportunity is yours! What a gracious path opens before you! *O Lord, how wonderful are Thy blessings, how beautiful Thy temples! Let us enter in, to worship forever and forever....*

V

The Mists Disperse

HUMANITY sometimes thinks that all the good that happens in this world, has originated from itself, failing to realize that collectively and individually, human beings are only instruments for spiritual and unseen forces that permeate their earthly life. But the human has one quality that sets him or her apart: the possession of freewill and the right to exercise it. The human has power of choice; the human can respond to all that is good and lovely, or may turn his back on these things and by following the path of self, reap nothing but disillusion and confusion.

Perhaps you will query this? You may be feeling particularly worried today, careworn, anxious, fearful. If so, just pause and think; try to look back over your past years. Review the troubles and trials through which you have safely passed, remembering too your periods of happiness. Then realize how you have been safely brought through your troubles. Realize that God has never left you without help, never left you alone. Always, something has come along which has improved your conditions. Even if you cannot admit that your material conditions have improved, have you not learned lessons that have brought you some ease of mind, some mastery over self? Are you not wiser? And even if you have suffered loss, has there not been some development, some unfoldment of your spiritual nature? Through your difficulties, trials and sorrows, light has entered into you; your consciousness of a divine love and a guiding hand has grown as the result of past events.

It is therefore a mistake ever to fear the future when it can bring an ever-increasing consciousness of God, an ever-unfolding understanding of God and God's life. It is equally mistaken to fear death. There is no death! We are always saying this. Some, and perhaps most of you, think that you believe it. You say, 'Oh yes, we know that there is no death!' But you do not know it sufficiently. You lack the deep realization, and the spontaneous reaction that you should have towards eternal life.

Neither Death nor Separation

Establish in your mind that human life is essentially infinite and eternal; that there has never been a time when you were not, and there never will be. At this, you will ask, 'Shall we not get tired of this ceaseless round of incarnation? Even now, life is a burden!'. This is why God has limited your days in the flesh; you live on earth only for a few short years which you call an incarnation, and then you leave your body as an outworn dress, and go for refreshment to your true home in the spirit.

In daily life, you do not mind moving from one house to another; you may love your old house, but when you have had enough of it you are ready to go. So also you come to the point where you would like a new body; you are weary and tired of the old. Then God is kind and allows you to pass on. You are removed from an outgrown state of existence and move onward to the next state.

Once over there, finding a measure of freedom such as you had never before experienced, you can rise in spirit to enter upon a period of intense happiness far removed from the former ignorance and limitation of your earth life. Then, when you have rested sufficiently and have assimilated the lessons of your earth life, your interest in incarnation is quickened, and the time comes for you to go forth again.

Let us make it quite clear: you need never be separated from your loved ones. Where there is love there can be no separation. Love attracts love as a magnet attracts steel, and you are inevitably drawn to loved ones, both in the spirit and as you go forth to fresh incarnation. The same law operates in all worlds.

Truly, eye hath not seen nor ear heard the glories prepared by God for the child of God. Humanity's limited consciousness has as yet no power to comprehend these glories. Men and women cannot even realize the vast range of varied existence in the animal and human kingdoms, let alone the subtler etheric, astral, mental or celestial planes which encircle and interpenetrate the earth and will be their future homes.

People earn for themselves Heaven or Hell

When you pass onwards, your state of existence in the next world will largely depend on how you have lived here. If the appetites of the body have been grossly indulged, your subtler bodies will be correspondingly coarsened, and cannot exist in spheres of beauty and perfection.

Do not misunderstand us. You may pass on to an astral plane very similar to this. A kindly life well spent will express itself in serenity and beauty in the beyond. But if your life has been one of coarse vibration and crude appetite you will find yourself in similar conditions on the astral plane, and there will be a return to earth fairly quickly to continue the process of education and purification. Men and women learn in physical life to discriminate between the real and the unreal, between the worthwhile and what is worthless. As they learn to discriminate between the worthless things and the finer qualities of the spirit, they develop what is called the 'astral' body, which will enable them to enter worlds of very great beauty.

Yet while the ordinary souls of ordinary people—individuals of the dear humanity whom we love so much for all their goodness—may not know very much about spiritual law, they are kind to others, and to be kind one must be unselfish. Such people after death quickly pass through the lower astral places in a dreamlike state until they reach a brighter astral realm, where they meet their friends; not only those whom they have loved and thought lost during their recent earth life, but companions they have met and loved during former lives or previous incarnations. They go to what is really a plane of reunion. Those who are left behind on earth also have a right of entry to this plane, but only if they can put aside personal grief or resentment at any loss they have suffered. In other words, only if they can so raise themselves in spirit that no lowering emotions hold them down to earth, can they reach their loved ones.

On the plane of reunion, the soul continues with its many interests—such as music, art, literature or science, gardening, and making a beautiful home—much as it enjoyed them formerly; but every interest will become keener and its enjoyment more vivid, because the person's power of expression will be greatly enhanced.

This process of passing away from the physical body, of traversing the planes of life and then at the right time returning, continues usually for a long time; but not necessarily so. It is possible to make rapid progress through the planes and afterwards gain eternal freedom. Nevertheless, until the soul has outgrown its lower nature and the lower desires, it must continue its earthly lives; but once it has outworn these experiences it becomes eternally free.

Yet there are those who of their own freewill reincarnate in order to help and serve humanity. Some are lowly men and women who live humbly and obscurely among the masses. They have their part in the plan. Others are initiates, masters spurred by a high ideal and purpose. We would emphasize the love and tenderness of those Elder Brethren who have traversed the selfsame path that the younger soul must walk. They understand, and never spare their help to any soul labouring on the upward path.

Longing for God

When once the soul has quitted the astral plane of reunion in order to pass onwards and upwards through planes and places of a wondrous loveliness that are indeed beyond description, it becomes able to see, feel and know, to a limited extent, the love and glory of God. That is when that soul most realizes its own inadequacy, its own unworthiness. The intensity of the radiation from God brings about this revelation. 'Nearer my God, to Thee; nearer to Thee!' is now its one heartfelt cry. Eventually, its longing to approach that beauty grows so intense that it will do anything, or sacrifice all, to realize that longing. Then a teacher will come to the soul. 'My child', the teacher asks, 'you want to get ever closer to the heart of God, to become ever more like God? Then you must get back to earth to learn. This is the only way'.

You may not accept these words with your outer mind. Your intellect may doubt or deny what we say. Look deep into your heart, however, and there will be no doubting there. When you have learned to search the deeps of your innermost being, you will know that you want more desperately than anything else to be at one with your Father–Mother God. You will know that God's light is reaching you all the time. It brought you back again into incarnation; it will take you onward into greater light if you will be true to its guidance. *I am the light of the world*, said the Christ, speaking through the Master Jesus. *I am the light. I am the light which lighteth every human being to the kingdom of God*. One day you will accept this as an expression of entire truth.

'Underneath are the everlasting arms!'. Strange it is to find how many people refuse the comfort of those everlasting arms! Yet infinite all-enfolding love is an ever-present reality. God is everywhere, is in everything. There is no place where God is not; no human heart need ever be bereft of God. He suffers with men and women in the depth of hell, rejoices with them in the highest heaven. Is it not said that every hair of your head is numbered; not a sparrow falls to the ground without God's grief and mercy?

The sky over our world is high and clear, golden with shining light. Let us leave the shadows, and look up into serenity, peace and joy. Are we not children of the light?

VI

A Clear and
Golden Sky

Right Thought

WE WOULD impress upon you the importance of right thought, of thoughts of goodwill, of God thought. If this beneficent habit became strong in humanity, with all peoples earnest in prayer for the coming of goodwill and harmony, help beyond measure would go to the Brethren of the Star who are planning the future of humankind. Indeed, we are able to tell you that the light has already broken down some of the shadows, and that a clearer understanding is coming.

Nevertheless, there is still much to be done before people are freed from the shackles of their ignorance. We must all be of the one spirit. It is the spirit of love, the spirit of Christ. This is only attained by continual effort to be as God created and wills you to be—sons and daughters of the light.

We see a future when wars between nations will cease. We see an entirely fresh way of life opening for men and women, a state of being which today you cannot even conceive. But remember that all social, industrial, national and international problems can only be solved by love; by love finding expression in patience, forbearance, service—in a word, by people living in fellowship and brotherhood with each other. Already you are learning that the good of others comes even before your own good; so that out of sore travail and pain the spirit of brotherhood is slowly but definitely being born.

Throughout his or her life, an individual's thoughts are actively creating his or her world. The individual's thought of today will be externalized in his or her environment tomorrow. Thus, when people think angrily about other nations, and when that form of collective thinking becomes strong enough, war comes about, and this solely as a result of man's mass-thought externalized and made manifest. All human life is a process of thought. What you think about, you must in time yourself become. What the world is thinking today will surely come about tomorrow. Everything in your physical world has eventuated because it was first created in someone's thought-world.

We come into your midst bringing a love which we find inexpressible in words. We only pray that the Great Spirit of love will use us as instruments to convey to you a realization of the all-enfolding love and protection of God, of which you stand in so much need. We are speaking to you collectively but also individually, because we are aware of your fears, your anxieties, and of your heart's hunger. Would that we could raise you from the earthbound consciousness that so often imprisons you.

Never think that we cannot enter into your troubles, or understand the weariness of the body and the anxiety of the mind. Never think that we are unconcerned by your mental or material troubles. Every secret of your souls is known to the masters. They work as with one mind, in complete unison; but when they descend to the level of humanity each has his own particular branch of work. Yet at the highest all masters are *one.* This is because the master-mind is in complete attunement with the universal mind, where truth abides. Radiations of truth go forth from this centre to envelop the whole universe and every individual life.

The angels and the Christ himself are not so remote as you are apt to think. You have the power—even at this very moment!—to leave all to follow him, so that you can abide with him in his high estate. Try to remember this, more particularly when you are bowed down by material troubles and cares; for it is then that he calls, saying, *Leave all and follow me ... for I AM the way, the truth and the life.*

Men and women make such a mistake when they think of heaven as remote, as far beyond their attainment. Heaven is within every one of you, and you must learn to find heaven while you are still in a physical body. Then you will surely migrate to a heavenly plane, when you slip off your coat of skin at physical death.

You are never Alone

Never think that you are alone in your difficulties. We have in mind those of you who are 'up against it' at this moment, not knowing where to go or what to do. You are blindfolded, but only temporarily. Contain yourself in confidence and peace, longing only to be a servant of God, praying that you may be still, and await your commands. All is known to God and God's agents.

While no soul is left in isolation, yet every soul must pass through its initiation alone. Every soul must also pass from one state of life to another alone. It is this very aloneness, this mist that shrouds the future, which eventually forces the soul to progress.

At first, the soul is like a child thinking it is self-sufficient, believing itself able to accomplish anything and everything, capable of solving on its own the puzzle of living. Through loneliness, it discovers the true Source of its strength. Indeed, on occasion that soul will specially need to be alone; for when the long-blinded eyes at last open and the soul's expansion or quickening takes place, it must be in solitude. This may happen to you: perhaps in this period of bondage you are purposely being left to yourself in order to develop your inner strength and faith in God.

What is this faith? Faith is an inner knowing that God can never fail in goodness and love. Every soul must develop this faith in God: not only this inner knowing that God is good, but also faith in the God within itself. Encased as you are in materialism, you are very easily misguided. It is as if a descending shutter had blacked out your awareness of the spiritual life about you. That is why earthly matters seem to you far more important than heavenly. Your real self is battened down in the hold of your own ship of life. That ship is your soul, which is being tossed hither and thither on the seas of emotion until in your extremity you cry out to awaken the master of the ship, the Christ. On the instant, he arises and says, 'Peace; be still!'—and the turbulent emotions subside and all is peace.

Inner Worlds

It is impossible for you to comprehend eternity with your finite mind; but you can listen when we tell you that deep, deep within you can become aware of the existence of worlds of unbelievable perfection; and that as you learn to command yourself, your fears, your emotions, your anxieties, as you learn to enter into the sanctuary of peace, so you will see the glories of these worlds revealed.

The Revelation of John gives a description of the golden city with golden streets and gates inlaid with jewels, the New Jerusalem. What is this city other than a portrayal of the inner self, of the pure soul of the initiate? For here the initiate's form is symbolized by the temple, his or her chakras or soul-centres are the gates studded with wondrous jewels, and the heart of the initiate is the throne for the Lamb of God, the Christ.

So also in the Gospel of John you can read a clear exposition of the soul's long journey through mortal life and of the heavenly places which await it.

The earthly mind cannot yet comprehend these matters, for human understanding is limited by people's persistence in living for themselves alone. But there are some who strive to live for others, and an even smaller number who live only for God, in God and with God. Some, on occasion, can touch the hem of His garment. Then—*they know.* Truly, these things of which we speak are the real things both of your life and ours.

Break your Bonds

We, who speak to you from the spirit life, are full of love and compassion for you, for we see you in bondage, immersed in a materiality through which you long to break. My children, your prison is of your own choosing, and is in reality the very condition your soul needs to prepare it for initiation. We know that you are yearning for that knowledge which alone can set you free; that you are longing to feel that you are close to God. You want this knowledge so that you may be a better servant of humanity; and yet you feel that you are making but little progress. But if you could truly examine yourself in one year's time from now, and if you could better assess the value of your human experience, you would say, 'Thank God for all the experiences which have helped me to progress thus far'.

You have to take this progress on trust. It is better that you should be blindfolded while you are serving your probation here on earth; for it is your attitude of mind to your hardships, restrictions and problems which is the great initiator, and which will eventually free you—and not through death—from the limitations of the mortal state.

As you are on earth, so you are here in the world of spirit—in which your guides, teachers and loved ones live. They come back to love you, to try and help you and to lift you up when you are in despair.

Incidentally, when you can thus open yourself to receive the inner light, it begins to 'iron out the creases' from the physical body and your aches and pains depart. People grow old because of their unruly emotions, because of anxieties they permit to over-rule and thus possess them; they become sick because emotional stress in time overstrains the body. If you were always attuned to the Great White Light, there would be no sickness.

Brotherhood

This is the picture of your world with its human-kind that we would paint for you. We would show you that every human soul, low and high, is linked to others as in a chain of brotherhood. Over all is the guardianship of an unseen White Brotherhood composed of lofty souls who have humanity in their charge. It is possible for people on earth to receive communications from these Brothers and Sisters. Step by step the message comes down; while we are speaking we are aware of other influences behind us, making use of us to convey their truths. Behind and above again are other influences and yet others, and so on, through the spheres; from earth to heaven this chain of communion exists.

Every one of you has your own guide of your spirit as well as your guardian angel, and you can be helped beyond all your dreams if you will go with a humble spirit into the inner sanctuary and pray, not in a self-pitying way, and not for self-gratification, but that you may fit yourself to be a true servant of humanity. Before you is the example of the Great Ones who have served humanity down the ages. They were formerly men and women who felt and lived as you.

This then is your way of life: to live not only to enjoy yourselves but also to beautify, to benefit the earth and its people, and to help forward the spiritual evolution of all life. This is a responsibility laid upon each living soul by its Creator; because the whole community depends for its progress on each individual soul that quickens with God.

Rise in Spirit: a Vision

And now, before we close, we would raise you in spirit into the presence of Jesus the Christ. Visualize him, as he stands before you in all his heavenly glory, within the arc of the angelic hosts. He brings the message which has been brought by all the ancient ones throughout time: *children, love one another; love God the Almighty Eternal Spirit and all His–Her creation.* And in God's love you shall learn all the mysteries of your own being, of God and of the universe.

See the responsibility that lies with you, and what a glorious opportunity is yours! Do not allow the darkness of earth to deny you your birthright of entering into the life of freedom and happiness, of service and worship of your Creator, the King of Glory. Peace and a great joy be with you!